What Is Balance?

by Marima Faivre d'Arcier

Illustrated by Volker Theinhardt

VIKING KESTREL

6

7

8

Try another balancing test—this time with a ruler. If you put a ruler flat on the table it won't fall over, but if you try standing it on its end then it will wobble a lot! Even if you do get it to stand still, then one small knock will make it fall over.

Now make a ring of modeling clay around the base of the ruler, but don't let the clay touch the table. The ruler will stand up much more easily now. But if you stick the clay farther up on the ruler, you'll find the ruler starts wobbling again. Try it and see!

It's difficult to balance something large and heavy on something small and light.

The easiest way to balance two things is for the lighter thing to go on top of the heavier.

You can test these balancing feats for yourself if you make your own toy like the clown. You'll need an egg, a tube of glue or some melted candle wax, and some felt-tip pens for coloring.

14

Empty the eggshell by making quite a big hole at one end and letting the egg run out. Dry out the inside by putting the eggshell on a radiator or leaving it in the sun.

Put about a tablespoonful of glue or melted candle wax into the eggshell. Stand the egg up straight and wait for the filling to harden. This can take some time, so be patient!

Now let the egg stand on its own—where does the filled part of the egg go?

16

Now you can color or paint your toy. You could make it into an animal or draw a funny face on it!

Here's another balancing toy for you to make. The bird's body is made out of polystyrene or Styrofoam, and its wings and tail are cut out of stiff paper. Its legs are made from used matchsticks.

18

Draw and cut out the bird's body from the polystyrene. Then paint the wings and tail and glue them on the body. Stick the matchstick legs into the body and try to stand the bird up on its own. Why do you think it keeps falling down?

19

It needs something heavy to hang down below it and balance it. So take a piece of stiff wire, bend it into a curve, and fix it into the body.

20

Look at that! The bird will even stand up on your finger now!

21

If a car or a bicycle tries to carry too big a load, then it will topple over.

To load a van safely the heaviest things have to go in first, then the lighter things on top!

When the wind fills the sails of a boat, the boat tips over to one side.
The sailor has to lean over to the other side to help balance the boat!

This boat has a heavy keel which hangs down into the water. This helps the boat to stay upright when the sails and boat are rocked by the wind and waves.

Have you ever wondered what it's like to walk along a tightrope? To help them balance, tightrope walkers sometimes carry a balancing pole. It's the same sort of idea as the curved wire helping the model bird to stand on its legs!

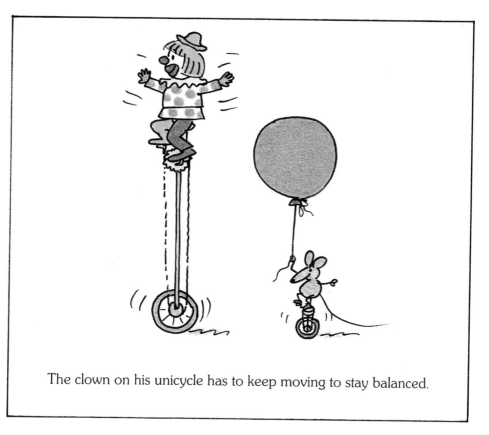

The clown on his unicycle has to keep moving to stay balanced.

And how's that for a balancing trick!

VIKING KESTREL

Viking Penguin Inc., 40 West 23rd Street, New York, New York 10010, U.S.A.
Penguin Books Ltd, Harmondsworth, Middlesex, England
Penguin Books Australia Ltd, Ringwood, Victoria, Australia
Penguin Books Canada Limited, 2801 John Street, Markham, Ontario, Canada L3R 1B4
Penguin Books (N.Z.) Ltd, 182-190 Wairau Road, Auckland 10, New Zealand

Translation copyright © Éditions du Centurion, Paris, 1986
All rights reserved

First published in France as *Les Équilibres* by
Éditions du Centurion, 1986. © 1986, Éditions du Centurion, Paris.
This English-language edition first published in 1986 by Viking Penguin Inc.
Published simultaneously in Canada
Printed in France by Offset Aubin, Poitiers
1   2   3   4   5   90   89   88   87   86

Library of Congress catalog card number: 86-40005
(CIP data available)
ISBN 0-670-81198-X